MW01308892

Will It Be Dangerous?

Who are More Prejudiced

White People or Black People

Kenneth Shelby Armstrong Th.D., Ed.D.

Fort Towson, Oklahoma

Will It Be Dangerous?

Who are more prejudiced?

black people or white people

Kenneth Shelby Armstrong Th.D., Ed.D.

Printed in the USA

Contents

A Story of the South

"Will it be dangerous? Could I get killed?"

"No! No! No! You're looking at this thing all wrong. This will be a great educational experience. Just think of it! A white graduate student walks into an all-negro University and tries to enroll. This hasn't happened to them before and I'll bet it throws them into a panic. After all, this is 1953 and it's time we get rid of this racial segregation and all the laws dividing us.

"We're in the Deep South and it's a perfect place for this kind of experiment. Atlanta University is here and it's a great negro school, but I'll bet no white student has ever tried to get into it. I think that If you would walk in and ask to be admitted that you just might be admitted.

"The timing is ripe. The whole nation is debating this segregation thing and it is just a matter of time until a federal law will be passed that will do away with Jim

Crow everywhere. You could be the catalyst to bringing it about."

"Dr. Stotts, I don't want to be a catalyst for anything. I just want to get my doctorate so I can get on with my life. I have already had four years of college and seven years of graduate work. I don't want to start another program no matter how interesting it will be."

"Don't be hasty. Think about it. You'll have your degree in a few months, but in the meantime you have some free time to experience a life-changing experiment."

"That's what I'm thinking about. This life-changing experiment could get me killed. Have you ever heard of the Ku Klux Klan? If they hear about this I will be dead meat."

"No one is going to hear about this. It probably won't even happen, but if it should happen you will come out OK. When you go in to get registered you should demand to be accepted. You should go in and threaten them with lawsuits and the federal government if they won't let you in. That'll really shake them up. Go for it, man. Think about it."

"You know that if they let me in they will be breaking the law. It's illegal for them to accept a white student. I could even go to jail. I could get killed. And what if your Dean heard that you were advising one of your students to break the law. It could get your fired but why should I worry? I'll be dead.""

"That's not going to happen, but if it does, I'll give the greatest eulogy at your funeral that anyone has ever heard. You will be immortalized."

"You're all heart, Dr. Stotts. You're all heart."

"Seriously Armstrong, think about it over the weekend. Let's have breakfast on Monday morning and talk about it."

"Armstrong, I've been thinking about our idea."

"*Our* idea? This isn't *our* idea. It's *your* idea. And I have some serious concerns about it."

"You worry too much. Think about the possibilities. This could start an avalanche of events that could affect the future of millions of people. You'vc got to do it."

"I'm not worried about millions of people. I'm worried about ***me***. Is it true that all negroes carry razors? I have heard some terrible stories about white people stepping out of their place and negroes stepping out of their place. I don't even care if the rumors are true or false.

"I just don't want to die before I get my Doctor's degree. And, what am I going to tell my father? He is already half convinced that I'm crazy. He wants me to quit going from one school to another and go out and get a job.

"Now, I have decided to try your idea but start working on that grand eulogy that you promised me. I have to call my dad and break the news to him. Pray for me. I will need it."

"Dad. Guess what I'm going to do."

"With you, Son, it could be anything. What are you up to now?"

"Next term I'm going to try to enroll in Atlanta University. It's a great school here in Georgia. It's an all-negro university."

"A colored school?"

"No, it's a negro school."

"Same thing. Why are you going to do a fool thing like that?"

"Well, it has a good graduate school and a great president. And it's connected with several other negro colleges like Clark, Spellman, and Morehouse. I think it will be a wonderful learning experience."

"Learning experience? Why do you need a new learning experience? Have you already learned everything they can teach you in Denver?"

"No. You know I haven't, but this is different. If it works out I'll be the first white student to enroll in an all-negro university in the South. I believe that in a short time the Supreme Court will rule that a negro can enroll in an all-white university, so I want to know if it works the other way around. I'll learn a lot that has never been written about in books. It's never happened before. This will be history."

"Well, I think you ought to be *studying* history before you start trying to *make* history. Besides, you should be working on your dissertation. Do you expect to stay in school the rest of your life?"

"If I could think of a way of financing it, I would. Why aren't you excited about this new idea?"

"Son, my blood pressure is up a little bit right now, but not in the way you'd appreciate. There are a thousand white schools where you can learn all you want. Why go off on a tangent? We haven't solved the race problem in the hundred years since the Civil War, so I doubt you're going to do it in one term."

"I know I can't solve it, Dad, but maybe I can understand it, and that's one step toward participating in a solution. I'll keep you posted. I'll be OK."

Atlanta was a new city to me. In fact, I'd never lived in a city that had this number of blacks. I made arrangements to live in a dormitory at Emory University, and my intention was to commute by city bus over to Atlanta University.

"Sir, does this bus go by Atlanta University?"

"Sure does, hop in."

The distance was not great, and I enjoyed viewing the city and watching the passengers come and go. Before I expected it, the bus driver announced the exit. I got up and went to the front of the bus to get off.

"Hey, you can't get off here; this is colored town. You're white."

"I have to get off here. I'm going to enroll for classes there."

"Well, you're not getting off my bus down here. Sit down!"

He shut the door and sped off down the street. I went back and sat down near the rear door. At the next stop several passengers rose to exit the rear door. As the last passenger got off, I jumped out the door before the driver had a chance to close it in my face. I walked back down the street to the University.

"Where's the School of Social Work?" I asked a passing student. I received no reply. It was as if I were speaking a language the student didn't understand. I tried again several times, but the results were the same. I was ignored. I decided to go into one of the buildings and ask a staff member or an official. I ducked into a side door of a nearby building and took the steps up to the lobby. An attractive young black lady stood behind a long counter, and I approached her.

"Miss, I'm looking for the School of Social Work. Can you tell me where it is?"

She smiled and said, "You've found it. What can I do for you?"

"I'd like your course catalog for this term, and I want to enroll as a student. I…"

"Sir, you can't enroll here. This is a negro university. No whites are allowed. I'm sorry."

"I know this is a negro institution," I replied. "That's the very reason why I want to enroll. The Supreme Court is just about to rule that negroes can go to white schools, and whites can go to negro schools. I want to enroll while it is still like it is."

"Excuse me a moment, please." She left the counter and went into an adjacent office. She returned and smiled at me a little less cordially than the first time.

"I'm sorry, sir. We just can't accept white students at this time. Keep in contact with us though. Maybe things will change."

"Miss, things have already changed; I'm here to enroll. There are soldiers at this very minute walking on college campuses, enforcing a negro student's right to enroll at a white school. Now, I probably can get some of them over here, if you insist."

"Excuse me, please." She left again to enter the same office. In less than a minute a dignified negrro gentleman came out and approached me. The young receptionist followed him timidly.

"Sir, I didn't get your name."

"I'm Kenneth Armstrong, sir, a new student."

"Mr. Armstrong, this is embarrassing, but we can't let you enroll. We're chartered by the State of Georgia as a negro institution. If we were to enroll you, we would violate our state charter, and to be sure, the governor of this state would shut us down for the violation. I'm very sorry, but these are our realities."

"Doctor, I in no way want to cause you or your institution any difficulty, but as you know, in some States this matter has already been adjudicated and the rulings have been against your policy.

"I believe that Georgia is no exception. I believe that the courts in Georgia will follow the precedents of other States and the Attorney General of the United States will give support to that position. I believe that they will support my right to attend school here no matter what the Georgia Governor wants. Respectfully, sir, I'm not leaving. I insist on enrolling just like any other student."

"Mr. Armstrong, I can't make this decision. Would you mind taking a seat and letting me see what our President says?"

I sat on the bench and waited. No answer came during the morning. Officials came and went, eyeing me apprehensively as they passed. No one spoke to me except the receptionist who offered me coffee or Cokes from time to time.

The lunch hour came, but the parade continued as if everyone forgot lunch. The distinguished-looking gentleman did not leave his office until about two o'clock. He came through the swinging door of the counter and approached me.

"Mr. Armstrong, please forgive me. I believe I forgot to give you my name. I'm the Director here. My name is Forrester B. Washington. Please excuse me now. I have to go to a meeting with President Clements and some of our trustees, and our legal counsel. I'll return as soon as the meeting is over, and hopefully we'll have an answer for you. I'm sorry to have you wait all this time, but I trust you understand the unusual circumstances."

Two hours passed before he returned. He came directly to me and invited me into his office.

"Mr. Armstrong, it is the decision of the trustees of Atlanta University to permit you to enter and visit classes, without discrimination. We will not accept your money for certain contractual reasons, but that is the only stipulation."

"But Dr. Washington, tuition costs are a part of the enrollment process. I insist on paying for my schooling just like the other students."

"Mr. Armstrong, you may write us a check for tuition, but I am instructed not to cash it. I'm going to put you in the hands of Miss Thomas who will enroll you and help you fill out all the papers. Welcome to Atlanta University."

Within a very short time it was apparent that Dr. Washington was the only one who welcomed me to Atlanta University. Most students were overtly hostile to me. Others were merely cold. My teachers were reserved and cautious, as if they had been carefully coached. I was sure such was the case, and probably by the school's attorney.

My first class session did not go well. I entered and took my seat. Immediately, as if on signal, the students near me got up and moved as far from me as possible. I felt like a small white island in a great ocean of hostility.

At my second class, I waited until everyone was seated; then I entered and sat as close to the center of the room as I could. Again, all those near me rose and moved away as far as possible, making a maximum amount of noise, pushing desks and chairs along in front of them. I sat alone once again.

The pace of hostility increased when we were not in class. When traveling the sidewalks from building to building, I was expected to move off the sidewalks to let the black students pass. If I did not move off on my own accord, I was often bumped off onto the grass or into an adjacent mud puddle.

Weeks passed, but conditions did not change. I remembered the words of Dr. Washington "to take classes, without discrimination." I now thought I knew the difference between the lofty promises of officials and the realities of everyday life. It happens on both sides of the street, but I was tired of the indignities. I didn't deserve the humiliation. No one would talk to me, so it was hard to learn much. I considered "scrubbing the mission," but held on.

School continued. I wondered how much rejection I could take. One Saturday morning, I wandered over to the student union to get a Coke. The place was nearly empty. I noticed one of the black students sitting at a table, reading a book. I walked over to him.

"Hi, my name's Kenneth. Can I buy you a Coke and ask you a question?" He shrugged his shoulders, and I took it to mean an unenthusiastic "OK."

I walked to a vending machine, placed change in the slot, and secured my two bottles of Coke. After all, this was Atlanta, the home of Coca-Cola. I walked back to his table and put his coke down in front of him.

He did not look up, nor did he say thanks. He selected a straw from the dispenser, put it in the bottle, and slowly sipped my treat. I spoke first.

"Can you tell me why nobody likes me? I try hard, but nobody will even talk to me. Why?"

Slowly he raised his eyes and looked at me. "Because you're different."

"Different? I'm just a student like anyone else. Why can't I be treated like a student?"

"Why can't we be treated like students at the University of Georgia?"

"But we're here. That's there. Who's going to solve the problem first—them or us? Do we have to wait to find out what they're going to do before we start talking and acting like human beings?"

"It's not that easy."

"Everybody keeps telling me that. I don't believe it. Am I so hard to talk to that we can't have a Coke and discuss a book, or a class, or a teacher?"

"They're suspicious of you. They don't understand you. You could be a threat to the school. You could be working for the government—any number of things."

"Then test me out, but don't freeze me out. Protect yourself, I understand that, but talk to me, even argue with me, but let's start somewhere. Here, let me buy you another Coke."

"No, it's my turn." He got up from his chair, walked to the vending machine, and bought two more Cokes. He returned to the table and handed me one.

"Thanks, Don. Your name is Don, isn't it?"

He nodded and allowed a slight grin to grace his face. He really was a handsome guy and probably would have been accepted in most universities up north without question, but not in the South.

"Where are you from?" I asked.

"Atlanta. Born here—never been any place else. They say you're from Denver. Man, I'd like to see the mountains. I've seen lots of pictures, and someday I am going up there."

"Come see me. I'll show you around. I never get tired of going through the mountain passes and following winding roads up a new mountain. I read somewhere that ninety percent of the highest peaks in the United States are in Colorado. If you like mountains that's the place to go."

"Did you really mean that part about showing me around if I came out there for a visit."

"Sure I meant it. You could stay with me. I have an extra room. Hotels are high out there and staying with me would save you a lot of money. Call me anytime. I'll leave you my telephone number."

Class was about to start. I waited until everyone was seated and then I entered quietly. I made my way to an empty seat next to Don. I sat down and nodded to him. He moved his body forward as if to rise and start the familiar ritual of moving his desk away from me—then he stopped, leaned back, and relaxed.

The other students, seeing the ritual being interrupted, paused and then relaxed too. No one moved this time. I looked at the teacher and took the pose of a quiet student intent on her every word, but inside I was shouting—yippee!

The same thing happened in every class. At last I had communication, and occasionally I was given a part of the sidewalk to walk on.

One day I was walking down the hall and one of the professors called me and asked me to come into her office. This attention from a professor was unusual, so I quickly went in and shut the door behind me.

"Mr. Armstrong, I understand what you are doing here at Atlanta University and I think it is a great thing. Just being here has caused a lot of debate among the faculty and students alike. Yesterday, I had an idea that I think you will like. So many of our students have unusual stories that never get told. I think you would like to hear from some of them. There is this one girl who has a great story. If you would be interested in talking to her I will set it up."

"Sure I'm interested. What's the story?"

"Well, I'll let her tell you, but I don't think many of the students know her background. I'll set it up for after classes tomorrow afternoon, if that's O.K."

"It's more than O.K. I really appreciate your thinking of me."

I walked into the empty classroom and saw this beautiful young lady sitting over near the windows. When she saw me, she stood and came over and introduced herself."

"Hi, my name is Marsha. I'm from North Carolina, and I get my Master's in Social Work in a few months. I haven't decided what I'm going to do when I graduate, but it will be in some job that helps people. There is a lot of need among our people, so I'm sure I will find something."

"Do you plan to stay close to home, or have you thought about going up North or out West?"

"Oh, I'm going to stay down here in Georgia, or I could go back to North Carolina, but not to my home town. Going home wouldn't work.

"Actually, going home would be impossible. I would love to be able to do it, but it's not in the cards. My mother has a beautiful home and I would be welcome to come home and live with her, but the secret might get out and it would wreck her life.

"You see my father is a white man and a very prominent banker in our town. I love him dearly and he has been so good to me and my brother. He loves my mother for sure, and she loves him. We have a great family, but if it got out things would get very sticky. Dad is the number one banker in the town. He actually owns most of the stock in the bank, but nobody knows that he has another family—and a negro family at that.

"Let me start at the beginning. My mom worked at the bank and was a sort of maid and janitor. She did most of her work after the bank closed and into the evening. My dad was a hard worker, and he often worked into the late evenings. Well, most evenings mom and dad were alone in the bank, and my mother is a beautiful woman, and so dad fell deeply in love with her. She returned his love and soon they had this situation.

"Dad was already married and had two children. His marriage was rather loveless, but he couldn't destroy it because of the effect that it would have on his children and the community. So they just lived with what they had."

"No one ever found out?"

"Nope. But, of course it was a difficult situation. Finally, my father said that they couldn't go on like that forever. Someone was bound to find out. So he asked my mother to resign. He said he would always take care of her and they would get together when they could. It would just have to be that way.

"Dad gave her money to build her own house. It is the nicest in our whole community. He insisted that it be as nice as the one where his first family lived. He put the house in her name and he gave her all of the money that she would need to live as well as his other family.

"It wasn't long until I was born and dad was the happiest man in the whole town. Then my brother came along and we had a wonderful family."

"Didn't anyone find out? Surely someone knew or suspected what was going on."

"No, I don't think anyone in the white community knew anything about it. I think probably some of the negro community suspected it, but they wouldn't tell anyone in the white community."

"My dad put both my brother and myself through college. He gave both of us cars and we both have a good start on life. It's just that we can't live in that town. It wouldn't work."

"Have you ever met you brother and sister?"

"Oh, I know them, but they don't know that I am their half sister. Both my brother and I went to private schools and since the law prohibits either of us from going to white public schools, our paths have not crossed very much.

I'm happy with the situation as it is and my brother has adjusted. He has had more problems with the situation than I have. Of course, mom is just grateful to have dad, even if it is not an every-day thing."

"If you marry, are you going to tell your husband about your family?"

"I've given that a lot of thought. I would have to trust a man an awfully lot before I would be that open with him. I just know that someday I will find a man with some common sense. I just hope that he will be as nice as my dad—not white, but nice."

I thanked the teacher for setting up the interview. She responded by saying that the school had an amazing collection of stories. Most stories were not as uplifting as Marsha's, but they all showed how negroes face their problems and over-come most of them.

One day I was in the library studying, when I saw a beautiful white woman come in and sit at one of the study tables. She brought out some books and started making notes in a sort of journal that she carried. I thought how strange her whiteness was in that context.

I left the library and went to see one of my favorite teachers. She was in her office and nodded for me to come in. She continued to work until she got to a convenient stopping place. Then she turned to me and asked "What can I do for you, Mr. Armstrong."

"Mrs. Marson, I thought I was the only white person here, but just a while ago I was in the library and I saw this white woman come in and start studying. I'm sure she was a student, but she was white."

"Oh that was probably Marie. She is a negro, but she can easily pass for white. You would be interested in her story, but I doubt that she will talk to you. A few years ago, after she graduated from college, she decided to go up north and ***pass***. She easily got a job as secretary at a large law firm.

"One of the young lawyers fell madly in love with her and it wasn't long before they got married. Not long after that she found that she was pregnant. She experienced morning sickness and she knew she had to tell her new husband that she was pregnant. And she knew that she had to warn him about being negro since she could not know what color the child would be. In these cases it is possible for a white-looking woman to give birth to very dark-skinned baby.

“Well one morning after a bout of morning sickness she told her husband that she was a negro and she was pregnant. Her loving husband shouted for her to get out of the condo and never come back. He pushed her out the door without a coat or without money

“Of course she was stunned. She went back to the door and tried to get in, but it was locked and he was inside shouting for her to get out and go away. She was crying and stumbled around but finally found a bus station.

“She went in and talked to one of the ticket agents and told him of her predicament. The bus people let her call her mother in Georgia who wired her some money for a ticket back to Atlanta. She cried her way home.

“When she got over the shock she decided to return to school and get a degree in social work so she could get a job helping other young people in trouble.

“She is about to complete her first year. Right now she hates all white people. I doubt that she will even talk to you, and sometimes when I hear stories like her's I agree with them. You white people are not so white inside. And we must forgive you, but we have not yet found a way to do that.

"Forgiveness is so important. We all have grievances of one kind or another—real or imaginary—and until we can find a way of forgiving and have a way of knowing that we too are forgiven, we cannot have the true freedom which we are all seeking.

"That's why religion is so important. That's why I say the Lord's Prayer every morning when I wake up. I pray 'forgive me my trespasses even as I forgive those who trespass against me.' When I go to church I ask for forgiveness, and I remember that I have been forgiven by someone who has the power to forgive. And that gives me a new beginning. I wish everyone knew that truth."

I had developed a habit of spending my Saturday mornings in the student union, where I usually met with Don. I got a lot of my negro education from Don. He was a good source of information about nearly anything.

"Armstrong, you know what you ought to do? Your experiment will not be complete without spending a Friday evening at Grady Memorial Hospital downtown. You ought to go to the emergency room there on a Friday or Saturday night and see what negro life is all about."

Without discussing it further, I decided to do exactly that and I did. I arrived at about seven o'clock one Saturday evening and already the place was filling up. I estimated that there were at least fifty negroes milling around waiting to be served.

I noticed a line of negroes at one of the doors and nearly everyone in that line was bleeding from one spot or another. Towels were wrapped around arms and legs but they did not hide the issue of blood underneath. I asked one man what the line was. He told me that it was the *sewing* room.

"That's where you go to get sewed up after you get into a fight with someone who has a handy razor on him. A lot of times after a guy gets his check on Friday night he buys a load of whiskey and gets drunk. Then he gets into a fight with his wife or girlfriend and she brings our her razor and carves him up. Or maybe it is one of his neighbors who does it. At least all of those people in the line probably have liquor on their breaths and blood oozing out from some where. It happens every Saturday and Sunday. They never learn."

It looked like a parade. People coming in with all kinds of wounds. They brought in an older negro woman who had fallen down a flight of stairs. She had broken ribs, and limbs, but she held on to her bottle of liquor. Even after falling down a flight of stairs the bottle was not broken. She was, but she held the bottle firmly and would not let it go.

I saw a man come in on a stretcher. Someone had shot him in the stomach with a shotgun. Looking down into a bloody mass of intestines did not go well with my composure. I went outside and threw up my dinner, but, that was not the end of it.

Every few minutes a new catastrophe dripping in blood came through the door. I had never seen anything like it in my whole life. I don't want to spend another Saturday night like it. There were no white people in the place. Perhaps they had their own private place of refuge in a more respectable part of the city. I went home to bed to dream of what I had seen on just one ordinary Saturday evening at Grady Memorial Hospital.

On Sundays I went to church. It was a life-long habit that I had developed largely because my father was a preacher and I was expected to go to church every time the doors opened for service.

I chose the First Methodist Church in downtown Atlanta. It was an impressive church. The services lasted only one hour. The sermons were only twenty minutes long. The choir was disciplined and trained. The people were friendly. I felt welcome and it gave me some time to meditate about the week past.

I asked Don if he went to church, and he replied that it was not a habit with him. He said he went with his mom sometimes. She attended the Wheat Street Baptist church. He thought I would enjoying going there. I did. What a great experience!

I arrived shortly before eleven o'clock and the service was in full swing. The sanctuary was round and had a balcony that circled the outside walls. The pews were also arranged in a circle around a large platform and a pulpit.

There were three choirs. One choir of perhaps 100 people was located behind the pulpit. A second choir was located in the balcony to the right of the pulpit. It was a bit smaller, but it made its presence known. A third choir was also in the balcony but facing directly at the pulpit. Down below the pulpit was an orchestra. There must have been 50 members in it.

And the music was grand. I have never heard music like the choirs, orchestra, and congregation produced. And the music went on. There were songs that the entire congregation sang, including me. There were special solos and quartets. Following many of the songs, the congregation would jump up and shout Amen and Hallelujah. Talk about *soul* music—it was there and they had it deep down. I don't believe that I have ever visited a church service that I enjoyed more than that one.

The sermon was also spectacular. The preacher was an older gentleman and he looked like a prophet. His sermon went on for an hour, but it seemed like it was only about fifteen minutes. Believe me. No one got bored during that sermon. It was punctuated with peace, promise, hope, praise, and he even mixed in a little hellfire and damnation. It was magnificent.

Even though the service was lengthy, I determined that I would return. It was well after one o'clock when the service was over, but I had found my church home. I returned many times.

One Sunday morning, they announced that it was to be a communion service. I sat in the back of the circular sanctuary where the pews became shorter in length. My pew only held two persons but I had a view of the entire church. When they served communion, ushers came down each aisle in military step.

Every usher wore white gloves and each had a white towel draped over his arm. There was a silent cadence to their marches down the aisle. They took communion trays from a linen draped table located just below the pulpit.

On signal they all turned and went to their assigned places at the first row of each pew. The style of the communion was known as the *open cup* style. This means that a cup is passed down a row of worshipers in each pew and each person drinks from the cup as it goes down towards the other aisle. Then the cup's lip is wiped with the white towel that each usher has, and then it is passed back down the second row of worshipers.

I sat alone in the back seat so that I could ensure that I would not be drinking from the cup that others had used. But, just at the last moment a large negro woman slipped in beside me and sat down. It hit my mind that I might be drinking from the same cup that she would drink from.

I sized up the situation and computed that the cup would come to me first and then to her, so I relaxed. But, my computations went wrong. When the ushers finally got to our row the cup went to her first. I noticed that she had the largest lips, generously graced with slabs of bright red lipstick.

She drank from the cup and with a large smile passed the cup to me. You cannot imagine what was going through my head in that split second between her drinking it and my receiving it. But, like a good soldier I took the cup and drank it down. The lipstick was flavored and I did not die. I never returned to the First Methodist Church of Atlanta, Georgia. Once you taste wine and you will never go back to mere grape juice.

America in the early 1950s was in turmoil. At the beginning of 1953 when I was in my adventure at Atlanta University, Truman had just finished his term as president and Eisenhower had just started his first term.

The threat of domestic communism became a topic of conversation on the street and in the congress. A senator named Joseph McCarthy stirred the pot of fear constantly. He shouted that there were communists in the universities, in the labor unions and even in the government. He chased them whenever he saw or imagined them.

He had great concern that communism was infiltrating the black communities and if they gained a foothold there, great calamity would fall on the whole nation. In a sense McCarthy's power was insignificant, but yet he had enough power to spook the nation.

A part of his power stemmed from the fact that he was held in respect by the Kennedy family of Massachusetts. McCarthy was so respected by the Kennedys that Robert Kennedy named one of his children after him. This was at a time when a large group of Democrats were forming plans to get John F. Kennedy elected President of the United States.

McCarthy had developed a close friendship with the father of the Kennedy clan—Joseph Kennedy. He used that friendship to promote his campaign against the ***Red Threat***.

One Saturday morning while talking to Don in the student union, I asked him if there were any communists in the student body. He looked around to see who might be listening and when he was satisfied that it was safe to talk he replied that were a good number of students who were communists. He said that they had an organized club where they met periodically. He said that he had even attended some of their meetings but he had not joined.

"Don, I asked a couple of professors if there were any communists here and they all said that there was no such activity. Were they ignorant of the facts or were they lying to me?"

"Lying through their teeth. They know what's going on. In fact, I think a couple of the young faculty are at least sympathizers. I don't know that as a fact, but I'll bet it's true."

"What do you think about communism?"

"I don't think it will work. I don't know of any country that promotes communism where there is true freedom. Chasing someone else's dream is a dead-end. We've got to solve our own American problems with American solutions. But it won't be easy."

My undergraduate major was Philosophy and I decided on Sociology as a minor. Accordingly, I had taken a number of courses in Sociology. On reflection, I concluded that my time at Atlanta University had stimulated my mind more than all the formal course work had done.

As I got to know more students, and a few other students better, my skin seemed to darken a bit, and the skin of the other students lightened. In fact, Don said to me once, "Armstrong, your skin may be white, but your heart is as black as ours." It was one of the best compliments that I had ever received.

The semester was coming to a close too rapidly. Laboriously, one by one, I built friendships, and was given liberties—the kind you have between friends. At the student union, I was receiving more Cokes now than I was buying. My social calendar, once blank, grew to activities even with several faculty members. It was as if I had suddenly developed a tan—a deep tan. My whiteness almost evaporated.

One day Dr. Stotts called me and told me that he had arranged for Dr. Clements, the president of Atlanta University, to speak at an exclusive girl's college down at Macon, Georgia. He said that nothing like that had ever happened at that exclusive school before. Did I want to go with them/

Of course I wanted to go with them. Dr. Rufus Clement was one of the most prominent negroEs in America. His whole family was extraordinary. His mother had been named National Mother of the Year —the first black woman to be so recognized. His brothers and sisters all held prominent positions in society. He was really important.

Dr. Stotts picked both of us up at the University. Of course I sat in the back seat, but I could hear every word of their conversation. That one trip was an education in itself.

At lunchtime, when we were passing through a little Georgia town, Dr. Stotts suggested that we stop and have lunch. Dr. Clement smiled and said, "Where?"

"Any good restaurant will do. We'll find one somewhere."

"Dr. Stotts, you're in Georgia. Not one restaurant here will admit us. It's because of my color. Negroes will not be admitted. Find a grocery store and go in and buy us some bread and lunchmeat. We can eat in the park. You will also note that there are two small parks near the court house. One is for white folks and one is for colored people. That's where we will have to eat.'

"That's nonsense." Dr. Stotts exclaimed.

"There's a good looking restaurant, and I'm going in and insist that they let us eat there. Just give me a minute."

He parked the car and headed in. Dr. Clement turned around and with a broad smile said to me "You want to bet?"

I didn't and was glad of it because at that moment I saw Dr. Stotts come out of the restaurant with wrath wrapped around his face. It was a terrible sight to behold. He was mad. But we ended up with Dr. Stotts going into a small grocery store where he bought a loaf of bread and some bologna.

We sat in the negro section of the park and ate our lunches. I had never seen Dr. Stotts so subdued. Dr. Clement just smiled and took the event in stride with a long-learned response of grace.

When we got to the college the president of the institution greeted us and said to Dr. Clement. "Sir, President Eisenhower has been calling and he wants to talk to you. You can call him back from my office, I have his number."

Dr. Clement told us later that the President had asked him to head up a United Nation delegation to Indonesia, and he had accepted the assignment. I was still fuming about that little George town that wouldn't let Dr. Clement eat in its restaurants because he wasn't good enough to eat with the white people.

The college had prepared the dining hall for Dr. Clement's address. More than 500 young debutants dressed in elegant dresses stood as Dr. Clement entered the room. I thought that it was a great act of respect, and I was proud of them.

Before Dr. Clement was introduced, the young ladies served **afternoon Tea** to everyone. It was a really nice ritual and the ladies exhibited the most delightful decorum.

I still remember the title of Dr. Clement's speech. He spoke on **New Horizons in Race Relations**. I have forgotten much of what he said but I do remember a few things that he said. He said that he saw on the horizon changes in the policies of employment, new educational practices, and wide spread citizen cooperation between the races. The ladies gave him an enthusiastic applause and they stood at attention as he was escorted from the hall.

The trip back to Atlanta was another good seminar on race relations. I had always respected Dr. Stotts as an exceptional professor, but on the trip back he assumed the role of an exceptional student. I was impressed at his reaction to the thoughts and views of the great black man in the seat beside him. I saw that Dr. Stotts had become color blind and I recognized that I was being inflicted in the same way. I knew that

I was in debt—and that it was a debt that I could never repay.

Emory University was a great contrast to Atlanta University. The buildings of Atlanta University were nice, but they were made of brick. On the other hand many of the buildings at Emory were made of marble. The wealth of the South had migrated to Emory, while its buildings and programs announced that it was a place where the elite sent their children to prepare for life.

Actually, I had become more comfortable on the campus at Atlanta University than I did living at Emory in a very impressive dormitory. The daily bus rides between the two institutions had also become interesting. I began to be acquainted with some of the riders who made this daily commute. I even broke the law sometimes and sat in the back of the bus where I could talk with some of them. The bus driver surrendered his segregation rule and started to open the door for me when I came to my exit. Talk about progress!

But not all was about school work. On a few occasions Dr. Stotts called and invited me to attend a ball game. The city had attracted a major league team and Dr. Stotts was an ardent fan. I was not a huge fan of baseball, but it was enjoyable being with my professor in a casual environment. His excitement was contagious but even in this place I noted a racial shadow.

Dr. Stotts always had good tickets, but I noticed that there were no colored people anywhere in our section. Segregation ruled even at the ball park. In the far part of the bleachers I saw a collection of negro fans. In that section there was not one white person, and in our section there was not one colored person. A ragged wire fence separated the two sections. It just didn't seem right.

"Dad, how's everyone?"

"Well, we've been wondering about you. You haven't written or called in weeks. Are you OK?"

"I'm fine. I'm busy but I do get a little lonely every once in a while."

"Are you still in that colored school?"

"Negro school, Dad. Yes, every day."

"Son, I have an idea. When is your term over?"

"The first week of June."

"What would you think of my driving to Atlanta, picking you up, and taking a little vacation together? I'd like to visit some of the major Civil War landmarks, go on up to Washington, D. C., and maybe even go to New England and see Plymouth Rock, Concord, and Boston. We could drive over to Niagara Falls and drive through Canada to Detroit, then home. What do you think?"

"Fantastic! Are you serious?"

"Absolutely, let's do it. Give me a specific date to be there, and the treat's on me."

"I'll call you. That's a great idea."

The final days that I spent at Atlanta University were somewhat sad. A lot of students who had never talked to me before, on learning that I was soon to leave, began to seek me out and converse. I think I learned more about my experience in the last two weeks, than I had learned in the prior months.

Several faculty members who had never acknowledged my presence before, announced to their classes that I would be leaving and I would be missed.

The remarkable thing about my time at Atlanta University was the fact that no mention of my experiment ever reached the newspapers, radio, or television. I was prepared at all times for the possible visit of some reporter or government official. My time at Atlanta University was a breach of tradition and the law. It never happened. To the world, it was simply a non-event.

Recently, I have looked through my old papers to see if I had any record of my time at Atlanta University. Of course there were no transcripts. That was outlined by Dr. Washington at the very beginning.

There were no cancelled checks to show that I had been there. The solitary bit of evidence was my library cards issued by the school's library. Apparently the administration had not informed the library that I was there under extra-legal conditions. When I had applied for a library pass, the people at the library were not aware of the conditions under which I was admitted.

I still have the two library cards in mint condition. One is dated April 3, 1953. The other one is dated June 6, 1953. The second card indicates that my place of residence was "Wesley Hall, Emory Univ.", (which was correct.) It also said that the school where I was enrolled was the School of Social Work at Atlanta University.

The Registrar or Endorser of the card is signed in ink but is illegible. The beginning initials appear to be L. B. and the name could be something like Tedthick. The librarian had apparently counter-signed the card using a stamp in place of a wet signature. The stamp shows the name of Ethel B. Hawkins.

Another curious thing about my time in Atlanta was that I can remember no news articles about the efforts of black students to enroll in all-white institutions. It is true that Brown v. The Board of Education did not happen until 1954, a year after I was in Atlanta, but that eventuality was not widely reported in 1953.

Later, I became aware of Medger Evers' attempts to enroll at the University of Mississippi during the time that I was in Atlanta, but the news did not reach me there. Evers was named field secretary for the NAACP for the State of Mississippi, and was active in many civil rights actions to get students enrolled at the University of Mississippi, but mostly he failed to defeat the southern powers.

His efforts in this regard also included trying to get James Meredith into the University of Mississippi's law school. But that effort did not culminate until the year 1961—eight years after I had already been admitted to Atlanta University.

In l961, Bobby Kennedy called out 500 federal marshals to guard James Meredith after the federal courts had admitted him to the University. It has also been reported that 20,000 soldiers were put on alert to stop any action against Meredith's entrance.

On June 12, 1963, exactly ten years after my experience in Atlanta, Medger Evers was shot in the back and killed. A lukewarm investigation took 30 years to capture his killer. At last the media was getting active about reporting the segregation policies and traditions.

My entrance into Atlanta University did not bring about the dream that Dr. Stotts had. Perhaps it helped no one else but me, but that was enough.

Dr. Washington called me in to see him in his office. At that time I did not know that he was one of the giants of negro education. He had always treated me kindly, but we had never had anything to talk about of consequence.

"Mr. Armstrong, I wish I could be giving you a diploma or at least a transcript, but you understand that the laws of the State of Georgia in 1953 will not permit me to do what I would like to do. However, for your files I have prepared a simple letter stating that you were here and that you attended numbers of classes and events." (Recently, I did find the letter in some of my old files. It was dated May 8, 1953 and looks like it was typed only yesterday.)

I do remember that last conversation with Dr. Washington as if it were yesterday. He started out by saying that he wished that he could do more than the letter but he ended up saying, "This is all I can do, but I hope you know that you are respected and appreciated. Your presence has been good for us, and I hope our response to you has been valuable to you. Perhaps someday the laws will change and you can even come here and teach to a desegregated student body. I do wish you the best in your studies in Denver."

I hate goodbyes and I'm not too fond of greetings, but the anticipation of seeing my father again eased the pain of parting. I felt richer because of my time at Atlanta University.

The Long Trip Home

“Dad, it’s great to see you. How’s Mom?”

“She’s fine, andhe sends her love. She said for us to be sure and bring home all our dirty clothes to her. We really ought to fool her and wash them before we get home. Get your things. Let’s get out of this big city and start our vacation.”

We drove north to the Carolinas. Dad had already planned the route toward the important battle sites of the Civil War. I saw that he had done a lot of preparation for the trip. We drove at his usual breakneck speed, but it didn’t hinder our talking.

“Son, tell me about that colored school.”

“Negro school, Dad.”

“Whatever you say. Did you learn anything?”

“I wouldn’t trade the experience for anything. I had a couple of rocky months, but it turned around and ended up great. A few Sundays ago, I went to the Wheat Street Baptist Church and nearly converted.

"The service lasted two hours, but no one left. I've attended that church several times. I'm usually the only white face in a crowd of more than a 1,000. They have three choirs, one behind the pulpit, one over in the side balcony, and one in the rear balcony.

"When they get to singing, everyone wants to go to heaven. And preaching? There's no better preaching in the United States. The pastor preaches at least an hour, and when he quits, I want him to go on. A couple of weeks ago I went to a large white church in downtown Atlanta. I was sure that the preacher had preached an hour, but when I looked at my watch, he had only been going 15 minutes."

"Isn't it dangerous roaming around a colored town?"

"Yes, it can be dangerous, but it's getting dangerous anywhere you go these days. You can't quit living just because it's dangerous."

"Well, what did you learn?"

"I learned that the whites of this country better change, or our society is going to snap like a twig."

"Do the negroes have to change too?"

"Dad, the negroes have already changed. It's the whites who won't change, and they don't want the negroes to change. They want the negroes to stay little Uncle Toms and be sure to stay in their places."

"Boy, it appears to me you've come away from that school with a passionate understanding of the problems, but did they give you any solutions?"

"Yes. People like you are going to have to change."

"People like me? What kind of people like me?"

"Prejudiced. Southern. Conservative."

"Now let me see. Prejudiced? Yep, I guess I am. I'm prejudiced for Jesus. I'm prejudiced for Paul. I'm prejudiced for all the great saints of God. I'm prejudiced for living right. Yep. You've got me. I'm prejudiced.

"Southern? You got me there, too. I was born in the South. Nothing I can do about that. And I'm proud of it.

"Conservative? Yep. I think you've got me there, too. I don't think we ought to change anything until we know we've got something better. We ought to keep our values and ways of living until we're sure we have some better ones. You're right. I'm prejudiced,

Southern, conservative! I'm glad I've finally identified me. What are you?"

"I'd like to think I'm an enlightened citizen with a deep appreciation for some of the positions that the liberals have forced on this nation."

"An enlightened liberal, huh?"

"No, Dad, but I'm a lot more liberal than you are. So's Attilla the Hun."

"Are you as liberal as those young fellers from Boston? Jack Kennedy and his brothers?"

"I don't know, but they sure are getting the conservatives edgy. I just might vote for him."

"Let's see. There's Jack, Bobby, and Teddy. Maybe you could change your name to Teddy so you could be a real enlightened liberal."

"Dad, let's quit talking about the race problem and enjoy our trip. We're neither one going to change the other's mind."

For the next of couple weeks we visited the historic sights of the Civil War. We visited the nation's capitol,

Plymouth Rock, the Old North Church, Concord, and Lexington. It was the most enjoyable period of time that I have in my memory of being with my father.

I learned more about history, literature, and poetry on that trip with my father than I had learned in college. Sadly, the grand experience had to come to a close.

We awoke to the sound of rain. This was the day that we had decided to start our return home. New England was beautiful, but it was time to go. Dad wanted to see Niagara Falls, then travel through Canada to Detroit, and then home. We chose our route. It would be pleasant driving in the drizzle and mist through New England and northern New York, I thought.

All day long we drove in the rain. We talked about history, poetry, religion, and of course, there was always the race problem to debate, if things got dull.

We decided to drive through the night and switch back and forth on the driving chores. Darkness came, and the rain still fell.

"Watch out, Dad! See that man walking? That truck in front of us hit that puddle and sprayed the poor guy.

He's drenched. Why would a man be walking along a highway at night in the rain?"

"I know why. I've done it," Dad said.

"What are you doing, Dad?"

"I'm turning around. We're going back and pick him up."

We pulled off on the shoulder of the road and eased up behind the man. He stopped and shielded his eyes from the glare of our headlights. He was soaked.

"Dad, maybe this isn't such a good idea. This is strange country for us, and he'll sure mess up your upholstery. Maybe we better go on."

"And he's black. Isn't that what you mean?"

"Well, we don't know him, and if he has a gun we could get robbed and maybe even shot."

"Open the door, Kenneth, and let him in the back seat."

"OK. It's your car, but be careful."

I opened the door, got out into the drizzling rain, and yelled for the man to come get in the car. He stooped over to look in the car at my dad. He looked down at his muddy shoes and his wet clothing.

"Sir, I sure need a ride, but I don't want to mess up your nice car. Do you have any paper I could put on the floor and sit on so I won't hurt nothing?"

Dad put a newspaper on the floor and said, "Here, you can put your feet on that. Take off that wet coat and get in. I'll turn up the heater."

The man took off his coat. He was shivering from the wet and cold. He stepped in and leaned back against the warm upholstery. I got in and shut the door. The heater was blowing at full blast. My father turned around and stuck out his hand.

"Hi, neighbor. My name's Ernest, and this is my son Kenneth. What's your name?"

"John. John Mason."

"Well this certainly isn't the kind of night for a stroll. Where're you going?"

"My momma lives at Jamestown, and she's sick. She called me to come help her. I gotta get there as fast as I can."

"How long you been on the road?"

"All day long. I've come 100 miles since nine this morning."

"How much farther you got to go?"

"I think it's about 250 more miles."

"John, see that blanket behind me? Put it around you. Don't worry about it. It's old. I'm going to throw it away when we get home, but it's clean, and it will keep you warm."

"You sure, sir?"

"Sure, and just call me Ernest. Look, there's a hamburger stand. I'm starved."

He turned into the driveway of the tiny diner, pulled up to the door, handed me some money, and said, "Kenneth, go in there and get us six hamburgers and three Cokes."

"But Dad," I protested. "We just ate an hour ago. I'm not hungry."

"You do what I say, I'm starved. Six hamburgers and three Cokes."

I shrugged and got out to get the food. I noticed Dad left the car running so it would be warm for John.

"Here it is." I handed the bag to Dad.

"Now John, here's your Coke and two hamburgers. Kenneth, here are your two."

"Dad, I told you I'm not hungry. We just ate."

"Then give yours to John."

"Ernest, I can't pay for these hamburgers. I got my pockets picked at the bus station this morning. All I have is some loose change. I can't eat your food."

"John, you eat that food. I sure don't want to get in trouble with my momma. My momma was a very strict woman. She's up in heaven now, but she keeps an eye on me. She said whenever you have people in your home, you treat them right, you feed 'em good.

"A car's the same thing as a home. You eat that food. I don't want my momma mad at me. Here, I'm not as hungry as I thought. You eat one of these burgers, too. I sure don't want to make my momma mad. I'll bet you haven't had anything to eat all day, have you?"

"No sir, but I'm OK."

We drove away from the diner. I saw what Dad was doing. I think John did, too, but he was too hungry to protest.

"Kenneth, look on that map. Is Jamestown on our way?"

"I already looked, Dad. It's a long way south of our route."

"Well, we're going there anyhow. I've never seen Jamestown, and I want to see it."

"But, Dad, it'll take us about three extra hours if we go down there. Besides it's night, and it's raining."

"I don't care. We're on vacation, and I want to see Jamestown."

We drove on. John fell asleep. He had walked in the rain most of the day. Anyone would be tired. It was past midnight when we pulled into Jamestown.

"John, we're here. How do we get to your mother's house?"

John stirred and sat up. "Oh, you don't have to take me. I can walk. Just let me out anywhere. I sure appreciate what you've done for me tonight."

"No, John! You're going to get me in trouble with my momma yet. She wouldn't like it if I didn't take you all the way to the door. I sure don't want to get her mad."

John gave us the directions. It was an old part of town. The only lights on were the neons at the bars. The houses were old, two and three-story tenements, placed as close together as possible. Three or four abandoned cars were parked at the curb. An old pickup truck was up on concrete blocks.

"There. That's the house. The brown one."

Dad pulled up in front of it, stopped, and turned off the motor.

"Sir, would you want to come in? I don't think she has any beds, but you could rest awhile."

"No, I'm gong to make this boy drive a while. I'm going to stretch out and sleep. We'll do fine. John, I want you to do me a favor."

"Yes sir. Anything I can do."

"John, I have this ten-dollar bill I want you to manage for me. I want you to take it and use if for a while, yourself, and sometime when you see somebody down on his luck, I want you to give 'em $10. Will you do that for me?"

"But Ernest, I'll make it."

"I know you will, but if you'll take this money and use it if you need it, then pass it on, you'll be doing me a personal favor. Just tell them that it's from Ernest Armstrong."

"God bless you, Ernest. I won't forget. Thank you for everything."

"Well, tonight when you say your prayers, you tell God to tell my mother what I did. I sure don't want her mad at me."

I got behind the wheel, and we drove through the darkened streets.

"Dad, this sure is an awful section of town."

"Not so bad. I'll bet more prayers were sent up to God from down here tonight than up in the Yankee section. If I really needed help, I'll bet I could get it easier on this street than Plaza Avenue up there. A lot of God's favorite people live down here."

"Dad, I saw what you were doing with John. You dropped your education and put on that down-home accent all the time John was in the car. You're a sly old fox."

"No, I just know his language, and I talked to him in his own language. He needed our help, and he appreciated it. We're going to have to remember him in prayer. You know, he sure was lucky that a couple of good enlightened liberals came by to help him. He'd sure have been in a fix if we'd been prejudiced, Southern, conservatives.

"Yes, sir. He sure was lucky. Now I'm going to sleep. You wake me when we get there. Good night, Teddy."

I fumed!.

View Point

Every book has a View Point. Each book is written
at some place in time,
by an author who was of a certain age and sex,
with parents who worked at certain jobs,
in a rural, urban or suburban setting,
following a plethora of experiences.

In addition, the readers of a particular book, brings of their own, a multitude of unique characteristics that make the book that they are reading an entirely different book from the book that the author had in mind. This book is no exception. It is written uniquely and will be read uniquely.

About half way through the writing of this book, I discovered something that surprised me in a way that made a difference in my thinking as I completed the book. I will share with you my discovery, but it is only given to illustrate the commonalities or differences of particular points of view in both the reader and the writer. In America the subject of race is thought about and discussed almost always with the shadow of Dr. Martin Luther King in the background. I have never met Dr. King, but he is there at my shoulder—powerfully there. I had not thought about his influence on my life before, but unknowingly he has influenced me and all Americans more than we know because of his dedicated viewpoint about race.

In my case the similarities of our experiences were striking. I had not seen them before, but they erupted as I studied the problems of race in America. I am certainly aware that the similarities that I found with the experiences of Dr. King are unique and the average person will have a different set. Perhaps, this differentiation will help others to broaden their understandings of the problems that we face today. The way it ***was***, can be a benchmark for the way it ***is***.

Both Dr. King and I were born just before the start of the Great Depression—the late 1920s. He was born two years after I was born, but our youths were much the same.

His father was a preacher and so was mine. Both were noted for having a special skill in preaching, and both lived in parsonages that were not luxurious. Even having enough food to eat is a memory that one always holds.

Both Dr. King and I were educated in segregated schools. I went to an all-white school, and Dr. King went to an all-black school. I believe that our segregated educational experiences affected us throughout our lives.

Dr. King was a precocious student and he skipped the 9th grade. On the other hand I was not precocious. I was just lucky, and I skipped the 10th grade.

In addition. Dr. King skipped the 12th grade as well and went straight into college. He never earned a high school diploma. I, on the other hand, was just lucky again and I also skipped the 12th grade and never earned a high school diploma.

Both Dr. King and I attended Christian-founded colleges. Both of these colleges were located in States that had Jim Crow Laws.

Dr. King majored in Sociology and graduated from Morehouse College in Atlanta, Georgia in 1948. I attended Bethany Peniel College in Bethany, Oklahoma majoring and minoring in Philosophy and Sociology, and I also graduated in 1948.

Dr. King went on to seminary in a northern State and received his doctorate in 1955. I took a slightly longer journey toward my doctorate. I took an M.A. in philosophy at the University of New Mexico, then I went to Nazarene Theological Seminary where I earned a B.D. in Philosophy and Theology.

I spent a year at the University of Kansas studying Sociology and Human Relations. I continued my Education at the University of Denver and received a doctorate in Higher Education. At the same time, I received a doctorate in the Sociology of Religion in 1958.

Dr. King was leading the Montgomery-Alabama-Bus boycott at about the time I was a student at Atlanta University. I followed him closely in the newspaper reports. In 1963, he led the March on Washington, D.C. and in 1963 I was teaching in a Christian college in the Republic of South Africa.

The point of recounting these similarities is to say that our experiences tend to direct our viewpoints. Individuals raised in the ghettos in New York will probably see the race problems differently than will a person raised in Atlanta, Georgia, or Enid, Oklahoma.

Young people raised in Ferguson, Missouri will see solutions to race problems differently from persons raised in Wewoka, Oklahoma.

And, of course, we ponder who will really develop the solutions to these problems. Congress? Billionaires? Professional politicians? No one? From whence will they get their viewpoints?

Life Before Atlanta University

Before I went to Atlanta University I was already at the end of my long journey to having my doctorate. All of my course work was out of the way. I had passed my comps. and my orals. I got my language requirements completed.

My dissertation was done and two members of my committee had already signed the final document. The third committee member had not yet signed so I went to talk to him about the hold-up. Graduation was only two or three weeks away, and I only lacked that one final signature.

"Dr. Ham, I was wondering if you had gotten around to signing off on my dissertation. Graduation is nearly here and I want to make sure that everything is done in time."

"Armstrong, I can't sign your dissertation the way it is. I'm sorry but I can't do it. I do think that the paper is a good one, except for one thing. Change that one thing and I will sign it."

"What's the problem, sir?"

"I can't accept your definition and use of the term, Sociology of Religion."

"But that's Dr. Stotts' definition."

"I know. That is where we disagree. I can't accept his definition, and he won't accept mine. I'm afraid you are caught in the middle, but maybe he'll change it to help you out. He won't change it for me. That's for sure. Go see him and let me know."

Dr. Stotts was adamant that Dr. Ham was totally wrong, and he said he wouldn't change his definition to please his incompetent colleague. He assured me that I had nothing to worry about. He would get the signature, but it would take a little time.

He said that Dr. Ham had several doctoral students that needed his signature so he would offer to sign off on those students if Dr. Ham would sign off on my dissertation. It was a matter of professional politics, but I would have to wait another year.

I waited through a hot summer and through the first term of the next year. Nothing had happened to change my status, so I decided to go to the University and try to break the log jam. My first stop was at Dr. Stotts' office.

"Armstrong, I'm glad to see you. I was about to call you. I have had an offer to trade teaching assignments for this semester with a professor at Emory University in Atlanta, Georgia. He is coming up here and will teach my courses and I will go down to Atlanta and teach his courses. Actually I'm leaving for Atlanta with my family day after tomorrow. This won't affect your graduation. In fact, it might help it if I get away from Dr. Ham for a few months. I'll keep working on him. Don't worry about it."

Of course I was going to worry about it. All kinds of things passed through my head in the few hours that followed his unexpected announcement. I went back to talk to him again.

"Dr. Stotts, isn't there something that I can do to speed this thing up? I have four months with nothing to do except to do whatever it takes to get my degree. All I need is one signature."

"I understand that. Say, since you have some vacant time why don't you go with me down to Atlanta? We can work on your program together. And, Atlanta has a major league ball team. We can go to some games and enjoy ourselves. It will be fun.

"I will get you space in one of Emory's dorms and you can even work with me in some of my teaching assignments. Think about it. And remember it is awfully cold, this time of year here in Colorado. Have you ever been to Atlanta? It is a great city."

I took a bus from Denver to Atlanta and that was an experience to remember. I had never ridden on a bus for such a long trip before. As we moved from North to South the occupants of the bus changed dramatically. By the time we reached Atlanta nearly all of the occupants were negroes. The panorama of passengers was a sociological study in itself, but nothing compared to what lay before me.

After Atlanta

The trip that my father and I made after leaving Atlanta was enjoyable, educational, and tiring. The time with John Mason in the rain was a topic that we reviewed hour after hour. I was convinced that my father had become more liberal during the trip than I had thought him to be. He certainly was more Christian. Of course, all in all I judged him to be the best father that a son had ever had.

Eventually we made it back to Roswell, New Mexico —home. Mom was happy to see us and even took our dirty clothes to be washed. But after a few days at home I was eager to get back to the University and finish my dissertation problem.

I went to Dr. Stotts office to tell him that I was back and ready to get to work on solving my problem with Dr. Ham. To my surprise, however, his office was open but empty.

I went down to the registrar's office and asked him if Dr. Stotts had returned from Atlanta yet. The registrar said that he had not returned and would not be coming back. He had received an offer to teach at Boston University and had accepted it.

I asked him what I was going to do about getting my dissertation completed. He told me that I would have to wait until Dr. Stotts' replacement arrived and go over the problem with him or her. I returned to my home in Roswell, as low as I had ever been.

After a few days of anguish I decided to return to the University and enroll in a few courses in the graduate school of education. By doing this while I waited for Dr. Stotts' replacement, I was gaining knowledge in a new field, but my doctor's degree in the sociology of religion was moving away from me.

When Dr. Stotts' replacement arrived I asked for an appointment to see him. It was granted but it did not turn out the way that I wanted. I was informed that if I wanted to get my degree, I would have to select a new dissertation topic and get it approved by my doctoral committee.

My new professor informed me that he did not know anything about the field in which I had written my first dissertation and so he could not evaluate my work. I would have to select a new topic in which he was informed.

Just selecting a new topic took several weeks but finally, I had something to work on. In the meantime I continued my graduate studies in the field of Higher Education, and before I finished the new dissertation I decided to get a second doctorate in Higher Education.

That meant that I would have to write another dissertation in the new field. So I started a second dissertation for a degree in Higher Education. Ironically, just before I finished that dissertation I was advised to stop work on it since my professor was moving to another university. I was informed that the new professor would either guide me to completion on that dissertation or direct me to a new topic.

Of course, the new professor preferred that I change topics into an area where she had expertise. I changed topics, and found myself working on my fourth doctoral dissertation and as yet I had no degree.

Tenacity is a powerful word, and with a little work and a lot of luck it can bring forth fruit. After a couple more years of work, I was awarded two doctoral degrees and found a job in higher education, and thus began my real education in a changing world.

I remember an interesting story about an older professor who was known to give his students the same test every year. He never changed the questions. Soon, it got around among the students that the professor always gave the same test and students copied the questions and passed them down to incoming students.

A younger professor went to the older professor and told him what was happening, and suggested that he change the test every year.

The older professor said he knew what the students were doing, but it didn't matter since he changed all of the answers every year. In real life that is what seems to be happening. The questions remain the same, but someone keeps changing the answers. Education must continue to be a life-long pursuit of changing answers.

Reflections

My time at Atlanta University was life-changing. But, as I reflected on all that I had learned and what I had personally experienced there, I began to recall other times of contact that I had had with negroes.

And the word negro has changed in general usage. When I was very young the polite name to use when describing a black person was ***negro***. Somewhere along the line, the name of choice was ***colored person***. After that ***Afro-American*** was the choice. Still later the preferred term was ***black.*** Today, all of the above words can be heard and I find myself using them interchangeably. I hope to be forgiven someday for this infraction.

I grew up in Oklahoma and one would think that I would have childhood memories of blacks, but I have none. I cannot remember having contact with a single black person as a child. Of course all of the points of contact that children have today, were restricted by segregation laws back then—schools, churches, and all public institutions.

When I was thirteen my family moved to Red Deer, Alberta, Canada. In Red Deer there was one restaurant owned and operated by a Chinese family. One day our family went to eat at that restaurant and as we entered I saw a sign in the front window. "No Indians Allowed." That sign puzzled me since I was from Oklahoma (Indian Country) and I had never seen a sign like that, before.

I began to wonder why Indians were not welcome. I could have understood if it had said no negroes allowed, but it did not. I remember asking my father why that sign was there. It was then that he explained to me that Indians in Canada were like negroes in the United States.

Then I wondered why neither were welcome. Did they have some disease? Would they hurt someone? It was a puzzlement to me, but after living there two years I accepted the act as being normal.

Then one day Dad came home and told Mom that he had a terrible problem. Dad was President of a small college and he had just received a letter from Barbados from a black person who wanted to be admitted.

The dormitories were full and Dad was sure that no one would want to accept the black person as a roommate. Later, he conferred with the Dean about the problem and the Dean said that it would be no problem. He said that the white students would be fighting to see if they could have him. The Dean was right. Everyone wanted to have him, but of course if it had been an Indian who wanted a room, no student would have agreed to accept him. Prejudice is so strange.

Recalling the above incident and working on this book stopped me dead in my tracks recently. It had never occurred to me that when I was in college in Oklahoma during the 1940s there were no blacks there. I simply had not even thought about their absence. I wasn't even sure that there were none there.

I called my old college roommate Dr. Val Christensen. Val had recently retired as vice-president of a university out in California. "Val, did we have any black students in college when we were there?"

Val said that he didn't know. He hadn't thought about it. But he couldn't think of any. Then he said, "Wait a minute. It makes sense that we didn't have any because when I left Wichita, Kansas to come to college, I came on a bus.

When we passed the State line between Kansas and Oklahoma, the bus driver pulled over and announced that we were in Oklahoma and all black passengers would have to go to the back of the bus. I remember that half of the passengers were black and so it was a real mess moving seats and baggage. So, I guess we didn't have any black students. I can't remember any."

To verify this judgement I called an old friend who had taught at a seminary in Kansas City for 30 or more years. Dr. James D. Hamilton had retired and moved to a small town in western Colorado. He agreed that we had no black students. He also offered that he had never even thought of not having black students until I mentioned it. That fact says a lot about the white mind in American society during that time.

Cuba

After graduating from college in 1948, I decided to get a Master of Arts degree in Philosophy. I chose the University of New Mexico in Albuquerque, New Mexico since it was where my family lived and which had a great department of Philosophy. One of my professors was Dr. Miguel Jorine, who had come from a high level position in the Batista government in Cuba.

At that time the Batista government was under seige from a young rebel called Fidel Castro. The local and national newspapers were filled with reports of the progress of this revolution. Some newspapers portrayed Castro as a great patriot fighting a dictatorial regime. Other newspapers claimed he was a communist and should not be supported by the U.S. government or any other government.

I enrolled in Dr. Jorine's class in political philosophy and each day he gave his report on the rebels. He hated Fidel Castro and his brother Raul. He insisted that his friend Che Guevera was no Robin Hood. He believed that the whole episode was led by a small group of Castro communists who had whipped up the poor and black population of Cuba. He asserted that true Cubans would not fall for the communist gospel, although he had resigned from the Batista government in fear of the imminent fall of the country into the hands of Castro.

A short time later I got the opportunity of going to Cuba to see the conflict for myself. Flying into Havana was a shock. Most of the beautiful hotels and resorts were boarded up. Shops and restaurants had their windows shuttered. The airport was full of wealthy Cubans trying to get out before the actual fall of Havana and the whole country.

I found a small hotel in downtown Havana and got a room. One could see that Havana had once been a jewel, but it had lost its glitter. There were few cars in the streets, and no policemen to be seen anywhere.

I rented a dilapidated taxi cab and asked the driver to take me out into the countryside. The tour was a grim one. Shacks were everywhere. The poverty of the people was evident. And it seemed to me that they were all black. I noted that there was a marked contrast between the poor blacks living in the suburbs and those that I had seen at the airport. The driver said that they were mostly from Haiti or from some other Caribbean island.

I asked what he thought about Castro and he shrugged and said that things would soon be better. I asked how far away the rebels sere, and he just said "Everywhere." That day was exhausting and I was glad to get back to my small room.

The following morning I decided to tour Havana again. I took a long stroll around the Embarcadero and walked through the back streets of the shopping area. Suddenly, I heard what sounded like a string of firecrackers being exploded, but no, those were gunshots. I stepped up my pace to go back to the hotel and the gunshots seemed to be getting closer.

Then, around the corner came a car with several men firing automatic weapons—spraying everything in sight. I ducked for a doorway and the car sped past and I decided that it was time to cut my tour short and get back to the safety of the good old USA.

I checked out of the hotel and a man in the lobby asked if I needed transportation. I told him I wanted to go to the airport as fast as possible. He asked if I had American money, and he quoted a price. I was glad to pay.

The airport was packed with Cubans trying to get out of the country. I pushed my way up to the ticket counter and told the gentleman that I wanted a ticket.

He asked if I was American, and if I had an American passport. I showed him what I had. I assured him that I would go anywhere as long as it was Stateside.

He said that only Americans were being permitted to leave, and if a vacancy in one of the planes became available he would call me. To my surprise he called me almost immediately saying that there was a seat on the plane that was just outside the door. I hurried out and climbed up a ladder and took the last seat. Within minutes we were up in the air, headed for New Orleans.

When we landed in New Orleans, we were surrounded by dozens of Cubans looking for friends and relatives who might have gotten out of Havana. They were all disappointed. Only Gringos escaped.

That night in my clean, safe hotel room, I pondered on my brief four-day experience in Cuba. I retained two strong images in my mind. One was that of beautiful buildings boarded up —empty and ugly.

The other image was that of shacks and black people caught in a trap of poverty and ignorance. They would be the pawns in the fighting. Many would lose their lives fighting for a cause that they did not understand. The promises of the rebels would never lift them out of what they had always known and suffered.

Dr. Jorine was right about the problem, but he had no solution. They are still seeking a solution. And if peace comes, the rich people will return and enjoy the comforts provided by a great supply of poor black maids, lawn boys, and chauffeurs. And I still do not know of a solution.

The United States Army

Near the end of my sophomore year in college I was drafted into the United States Army. The year was 1945 and it was not yet determined that we would or could win the war. Basic training in Little Rock, Arkansas was cut short so that we could go over to Europe to help out. The Battle of the Budge was raging. The casualties were massive. We were the first in line to be fed into the slaughter pen.

But before we could be shipped out, the war in Europe was ended and shortly after that two atomic bombs were dumped on Japan. The war was over. I remember vividly the celebrations all over America. But my war was not over. The US Army had plans for me and my buddies.

Somewhere in the high echelons of the Army it was decided to bring the war weary soldiers home as soon as possible. It was one of the good decisions that the Army made. That meant, however, that a new supply of soldiers would have to be immediately dispatched to Europe and Japan to serve as occupational forces.

My army unit, composed of men from Oklahoma, Arkansas, and Brooklyn was sent to Seattle where we were put on the USS General Blatchford destined for some obscure South Pacific island or perhaps Japan. We had no idea where we were going. There was not much glee expressed as we trudged up the gangplank with all of our worldly possessions on our backs. Even after three weeks on the ocean we had no idea of our intended destination.

The composition of the 3,800 soldiers on board was a recipe for conflict. The 3,600 white soldiers from Oklahoma, Arkansas, and Brooklyn had the basis for conflict, but an added 200 black soldiers guaranteed an exciting voyage.

Segregation in the Army was strictly enforced but it was not operative between Brooklynites, Okies and Arkies. It should have been. In addition, the close proximity of 200 black soldiers aboard became the catalyst for minor and not-so-minor skirmishes. Every day was an opportunity for the clashes of egos and ids.

The focal point of contention was what the sailors called the **Gedunk.** It was something like what soldiers called a **PX**. The supply of articles made available was limited, but sufficient for the needs and minor wants of the soldiers—cigarettes, cokes, candy bars, and ice cream. All you needed was to wait in a long line each morning and have money in your pocket. The time was not a problem, but money was.

As soon as it was known that you had money, you became a banker without—lien or recourse. After three weeks of lending and borrowing, few had anything left.

But getting to the Gedunk became a problem. You would get into the back of the line to the Gedunk and it never seemed to move. Someone found out that the black soldiers had devised a way of bucking the line. The black soldiers would let other blacks get into the front of the line, making the white soldiers waiter what seemed like forever.

Eventually, it was discovered what the blacks were doing and fights erupted. The Marines, who were the law and order on the ship, brought their clubs in to establish temporary peace. In fact, at one point the Marines themselves were attacked by the blacks and an emergency was called. The Gedunk was closed and all soldiers were confined to their bunks for a period of time.

The temporary truces established by the ship's officers were short lived and it was rumored that when the ship arrived in Japan, there were fewer blacks and whites who debarked than there were when we embarked at Seattle. Of course, we all know how much actual truth exists in rumors, but some rumors are more believable than others.

Eventually, all who landed were assigned to army units which performed all kinds of functions. I was assigned to Sixth Army Headquarters where we never saw a black soldier.

The blacks went to motor pools and quartermaster units. The whites went to headquarters. I learned nothing about black-white relations during that year. I was too busy worrying about relationships with the Japanese and no blacks were around.

I did, however, hear the rumor that Japanese women preferred the black soldiers to the whites. I did not pursue the study of that phenomenon. I just wanted to go home. In 1946 I was back in college—my all-white college.

The Republic of South Africa

Eventually, I found a good job in teaching and administration at Pasadena College, Pasadena, California was a great place to live, except for the terrible smog.

Four years into that job I received a letter from an old classmate of mine. He was head of a small college in Johannesburg, South Africa. Although he was the administrative head, his largest responsibility was teaching. He had been doing that for nearly a decade and he was tired.

The reason for his letter was to ask if I would come to Africa and take his job for a year while he came back to the States to refresh himself, and to acclimate his family back into the American stream. I pondered the idea for a few days and since I am somewhat of an adventurer, I replied. "Sure, why not?" Then he explained to me that the students were all white. No blacks were allowed.

There were many things to ponder, but adventurers don't always consider all of the factors that are in a venture and I certainly did not. The year was 1963 and it was almost Christmas time, which I would miss with my family if I accepted the proposal. Finally, it was decided that the family would wait in Pasadena until Summer and then come. Otherwise, the year would interfere with my two children's education.

And so I was off for my next adventure. I decided to spend three weeks going through Europe to Africa—London, Paris, Rome, Athens, Cairo, Nairobi. That was a great experience.

Slowly, it dawned on me that I was leaving a country that was predominantly a white country with a small population of non-whites, and going to a country that was predominantly a black country with a small population of whites. I learned that for every white person in South Africa, there were 19 blacks.

This was like my experience of going to an all-black university. I soon found out that there were many parallels; however one thing was different. In South Africa, the minority (whites) ruled the country with a strong fist. The minority (mostly blacks) had surrendered to the unfairness of the population distribution.

But not all surrendered. I soon found out that there was a growing tide of rebellion in the country. Safety was not a guarantee, especially in the small towns and rural areas. One had to be on alert at all times.

The name of Nelson Mandela became a familiar name to me. I had never heard of him, but I learned about him from the white community, who considered him to be an ogre of some kind. He was greatly hated and I adopted that attitude without thinking more deeply about it.

Many years later, I discovered that Dr. Martin Luther King considered Mandela to be one of the great humanitarians in history. On reflection I had to agree with Dr. King. My attitude changed.

But, at the time, many of the whites were fearful of the possible revolt. I was told that among the black people there were already plans, that on signal, the black population would overpower the whites, and most whites would be killed.

The school had hired a black lady to take care of me while I was there. Anna was a good cook and a great house keeper. She was friendly and had a bubbly personality. One day, I asked her if there was a plan to take over the country. I said that I had heard that when a certain signal was given, all of the black servants were to rise up and kill their masters. I asked her if it was true.

She said, "No master, I would never kill you. I love you. I am supposed to kill the family next door and their servants are supposed to kill you." It was a very neat arrangement. Thankfully, the plan was never carried out because of the leadership of Nelson Mandela and some very wise Dutch and English leaders.

I liked nearly everything about Anna and found out that I was greatly saddened on planning my leave of the country. It had been only a year, but the bond was tight.

The word *nearly* in the previous paragraph was used intentionally. One of the things about South Africa when I was there is that they didn't put paper around their bread. They merely put a small strip around the middle of the loaf when you bought it.

One day when I was on my way home, I passed Anna who was coming from the tea room where everyone bought their bread. Anna was walking along under the hot sun, sweating profusely. And she was carrying the bread that she had just bought under her arm—that is, under her ***arm pit***. The sweat was running down her arm and I could only imagine what was happening to the loaf of bread.

From then on, I cut off the crust from each slice of bread and sort of breathed a prayer to protect me from little germs which might have found a home in the bread that I was about to eat. I don't think that she could understand why I didn't eat the crust. It was the best part of the bread so, she ate it herself. We both continued in good health.

One enjoyable thing to me was to take my Holden automobile (which was built in Australia) and visit as many places as I could. I took tours to Swaziland, Mozambique, North Rhodesia, and South Rhodesia. In addition I visited Durban, Cape Town, Pretoria and places which I cannot now spell.

I also liked to visit the villages in out-of-the-way places. Whenever I would drive into a small village, instantly the children and dogs would converge on me, laughing, shouting, and barking. I could never get over the fact that each village held so much joy without having all the things that we in America had to have in order to make us happy.

I think that it was Carl Rogers who said that "the greatest thought of the twentieth century is, that man by changing his inner attitudes, can actually change the outer circumstances of his life."

I am convinced that the solution to most of our racial problems lies in the attitudes that we have developed. If we would only seek to change our attitudes about those whom we have to live with it would certainly act to change them.

If we would change our attitudes about the things we have, or don't have, our outer circumstances would begin to change. I am convinced that it is all about attitudes which we *can change*, although sometimes with great struggle.

In South Africa the Dutch-English domination of society made it difficult to communicate about black and white relations. During the day the blacks were accessible because they were doing chores for the Whites. At night they evaporated and re-appeared in the large ghettos designed to be barriers to further exchange. I felt that it was much like America in that regard. Whites lived where they could afford, and blacks found their places in what was left.

I left South Africa, richer for the time I spent there. I went back to California and resumed my life with family, friends, a mortgage, and opportunity. I seized the opportunity and put my foot on the first rung of the ladder. I wanted to go ***up***, and I could because I was in America.

About ten years after I left South Africa I was approached by an owner of a chain of small newspapers. He asked me if I would like to go back to South Africa on a fact-finding mission.

At that time the government of South Africa was being hammered for its racial policies. The attack was coming largely from the American press. Their main concern was the policy of apartheid which was maintained by the South African government. The separation of the races in America was bad, but apartheid was impossible to accept.

The newspaper man said that the South African government had developed a policy designed to neutralize the bad press in America. They had decided to select certain Americans who were influence-makers to come to South Africa and tour the country at the government's expense.

The visitors from America were provided the freedom to go anywhere and see anything they wanted. Guides, transportation, and accommodations were to be provided by the government without restriction. The hope was that the Americans would return to their homes and take a favorable message back to the American people and neutralize the media attack or change it if possible.

I was asked if I would care to go to South Africa on one of the jaunts with all expenses paid. Again, I said I would go if I could see what I wanted to see without being controlled by a government agenda.

It was a great trip. The first thing that I received was a first-class round trip ticket to Johannesburg. The price on the ticket was over $5,000. I could never have afforded a trip like that. On arrival, we were taken to the best hotel in the city and after checking in we were taken to the best restaurant for dinner.

After breakfast the next morning we met two attractive young ladies who said they would be our guides for the next three weeks. We were asked if there were things that we would like to see, or people that we would like to meet. They said that they would make all of the arrangements. There were only three of us on this particular mission.

I indicated that I would like to visit some of the black colleges that the government had built for the black students. Also, I said that I would like to visit the black hospitals that were available to all natives. Their comment was "No problem. We will arrange it today."

At no time did I detect an effort by the guides to influence or slant our experiences. We made our own conclusions based on our own observations.

During the following days, we visited several black colleges and talked to resident faculty members and students alike. We visited a large hospital which I was told was the largest hospital in the southern hemisphere, and it was for black people only and without charge.

We visited the ranch of one of the elected representatives of the government. The hospitality was excellent. I could have imagined that I was in west Texas. The subject of apartheid never came up.

One day I asked to visit one of the suburban housing areas in which the natives lived. That was a traumatic experience and not greatly different from what I had seen in south Atlanta or south-side Chicago.

Three weeks and twenty pounds later, I departed Johannesburg and flew home with stops in India, Thailand, Saigon, Taiwan, the Philippines, and Japan. The long flights gave me ample time to think and review the events of the previous three weeks.

At the end, I came to believe that the government in South Africa was in many ways more compassionate and responsible than our government in my own beloved country. I was not certain that the people of South Africa would gain much by getting the power to elect its own government.

I remembered what had happened when Northern Rhodesia made the transition from white rule to democratic rule. I was there the week that it happened.

My Friend Tracy

It has been a long road since I left Africa. I have had many experiences with people, but few with black people. That is the way our society has become. We have learned to live ***apart*** without having ***apartheid***. But that is not really a very good way to live. Many of us believe that we must find a way to come together in a new bond of ***oneness***. But, will coming together be possible and if possible, will it be dangerous?

I always keep busy. It was the way of my father and I adopted it. When I was in church work, there was always a church that needed to be built or refurbished. I learned how to do that. When I was in education there was always a classroom building or a dormitory that needed to be built.

I used my head and hands to accomplish that as well. When I was in retirement I just found a house somewhere that needed some tender, loving care, and I gave mine to it. I was always thankful for the lessons taught to me by my father.

I think I was fourteen or fifteen years of age when my father took me aside one day and said, "Kenneth, I think it is time for me to tell you about your inheritance." That surprised me because I could see nothing that we had that was valuable.

"Son, I have three very valuable things that I am going to leave with you. I want you to keep them and some day pass them on to your son. For the first time, my anticipation exploded. He was serious.

"First, I am going to leave you a good name—Armstrong. That may not seem much to a lot of people, but to have a good name is a very valuable thing. When you tell people your name, stand up straight and stick your chest out a bit when you tell them that your name is ***Armstrong.***

"Second, I am going to leave you my love. It is a valuable thing to have your father's love. A lot of people don't have that, but I love you and will love you as long as I live. It is unconditional, too. No matter what you do, I will love you.

"Third, I am going to teach you how to ***work***. If you learn how to work, no one can ever starve you. That may be the most valuable thing that you will ever have. Many people don't know how to work and they live miserable lives. But, I am going to teach you how to work and you will be able to get nearly anything you need."

To say the least, I was not greatly impressed with my eventual inheritance, but I never forgot what he said. As I grow older, I can see that my inheritance is more valuable than I could ever have dreamed. I have it all.

At 88 years of age I go out and work every day. I find something to do that will make a difference for my family or for someone else. It is the Armstrong legacy. To the amazement of nearly everyone, my father was still working when he was well past 90. I want to out-do him, if I can.

I found a nice house around the corner from where I live on Lake Raymond Gary. It had the best view on the lake. All it needed was a little imagination and modernizing.

Next to the house was a large barn and it had a stunning view of the lake. I thought about it for a while and decided that I could covert that old barn into a beautiful house. I took out my pencil and paper and drew plans. I knew it would be a hard job, but it was doable.

First, I had to empty the barn with its decades of piled-up junk. That was a great job, but every once in a while I found a forgotten treasure. I found a box of old automobile license plates dating back into the 1940s. Then I found an old model T Ford jack that was a collector's item. There were also tools of all kinds and old kitchen pots, pans, knives and skillets. I had a great time just getting ready to go to work, but even though I had dirt on my hands, I had a dream in my heart.

One day an old black man walked up and saw me at work. "Looks to me like you need some help here." he said.

I looked him over and replied that I always needed help, but I could never afford to pay people what they were asking. "So," I said, "I just do it myself."

"Your problem is that you haven't seen me work. I've been working all my life and I have never been fired because I didn't know how to work."

I looked him over again and tried to guess his age. I am not good at guessing ages, but I thought he was more than 70. He wasn't very big and he didn't look very strong, but I liked his attitude.

"You want to try it out with me a day or two so we can see if you want to work with me, and so I can see if I can pay you what you're worth?"

"I can't lose with a proposition like that. Hand me that shovel and I'll start right now." And he did. He said his name was Tracy and I told him my name was Kenneth. It seemed to be a good workable relationship so the next day I told him that I thought I could afford to pay him $10 an hour if he could afford to take that. He stuck out his hand and we shook on it. In Oklahoma, that is an iron-clad contract.

Tracy was not afraid of work. He told me up front that he didn't know much about building, but he would do whatever I said. He said that he was eager to learn how to build a house from a barn.

I told him that we were going to use the post and beam system for our foundation. This system consists of digging deep holes, filling them with concrete and then putting a post on the concrete to hold up the beams on which we would construct our flooring. It is not rocket science, but it is arduous work.

I staked the places for all of the holes to be dug. I put them every four feet everywhere we would have a room. I bought a small cement mixer which cut down some of the work. For days, we dug holes, mixed cement, and set out beams.

One day I told Tracy that I could not work the next day so he would be by himself. I staked out 19 holes and told him to work on it and I would see him later. He assured me that he was up to the assignment. I was sure that he could not get all 19 holes done, but if he got half that many done I would be happy.

The next afternoon at about four o'clock, I went to the job site and saw Tracy sitting on a pile of lumber. He was mopping his forehead because it was hot and he had been working hard.

"Well, I got it done. I decided that I was going to show you what I could do and I finished all 19 of them. Can we start framing in the morning?"

"Tracy, you are making it hard on me. I never dreamed that you could do all that work in one day, so I am going to have to pay you more now. As of in the morning you will be earning $12 per hour." His grin stretched from ear to ear.

For two old men, building a 2500 square foot house is quite an undertaking. We had no one else, so just the two of us did what needed to be done. I decided once again, that retirement is not what it's cracked up to be.

One day a couple of young men walked up to the site and asked who was going to do the framing on the house. I replied that Tracy and I were going to do it. They told me that they could do it since they had been raised by contractors and had been helping their dads since they were kids. I asked their ages and found that they were 18 and 19 years old. I told them that I could pay them $10 an hour and they accepted it and started to work.

Everything went along fine for perhaps a week. Tracy and I worked together on some job and the two young men started the framing.

"Kenneth, I'm not happy. Ever since those boys came here things are not as much fun. I liked working with you, but I don't like working with those kids. They keep telling me to do things like go get a pile of lumber for them. They don't ask me—they tell me. I don't like taking orders from kids who have just come out of diapers. I was here before they were."

"But Tracy we need those boys. They have the skill to frame this whole house, so that saves us from having to do it, and you've never framed a house before. Try to get along with them if you can."

But, he couldn't put up with it and I didn't blame him. The inevitable thing happened one Friday afternoon. Tracy said that he had to do some work around his house and he wouldn't be coming to work the next week. I told him that I regretted it, but he had to do what he felt was necessary.

Before he left he asked if I was going to sell my old Dodge pickup. I had talked about it before, and he had said that he would like to have one just like mine. He asked if I would sell mine to him. I asked him for the price that he was willing to pay and he gave me a figure. Then he asked if he could pay it off over time. He said he could pay $200 per month. We agreed on the price and payment and my wife did all of the paper work. The truck was his.

My wife remarked several times later that Tracy was always on time with his payments. He mailed them to us with a money order made out in the correct amount. It was a good thing for both of us.

One Sunday morning I was reading my favorite passage of scripture in the Bible. It was called the ***Sermon on the Mount***. I had read it hundreds of times over the decades and it always gave me instruction and inspiration. On that particular Sunday morning it talked to me about doing good to the less fortunate of my neighbors. And the name, Tracy popped into my head.

I called my wife to come down and talk to me. I asked her what she would think about our forgiving the debt on the old Dodge and giving it free and clear to Tracy. Without hesitation, she said, “Let’s do it.”

During the week she did all of the paper work and so the next Sunday morning we drove to Tracy's house. His house was freshly painted and the lawns were mowed. He had a fence around his property and one could see the pride that he had in the place.

He was standing towards the back of his lot when I called to him. I was not sure that he could see who was calling, but he ambled towards me. I had not seen him since he had left that last Friday night, but he looked as healthy as always.

"Tracy, I've got something for you. Last Sunday I was reading the Bible about doing good, and I wondered what good I could do. It popped into my head that I could give you the Dodge and eliminate your payments. Here is the title to it and we have taken off the lien. It is yours and you can forget the payments from now on."

He took the deed and said "Why would you be doing this?"

I said "Because it is a good thing to do, and I am supposed to be doing good things."

He looked at the deed and said, "I'm doing O.K. I can make it without help." I replied, "I know you can Tracy, but this will make it easier."

He walked away, back to where he was when I arrived. He didn't say anything at all. He didn't thank me, or say anything else. He just put the paper in his pocket and continued what he was doing. I have never see him since that time.

My wife asked what he said, and I told her that he said nothing. It was a very strange reaction and I wondered what had caused it. I tend to think that it meant that he could not fathom anyone doing what we had done with no apparent selfish reason.

I believe that the decades of his life had told him that white people do not do benevolent things without a reason. I believe that he had been hurt so many times in his life that he had to keep his guard up from being vulnerable to more hurt. I would like to be his friend but I am afraid that we have both lived too long to reorient our prejudices.

Contemplation

During my journey through eight decades of labor and love, through hate and hope, and faith and forgiveness, I have developed some observations that should be examined. The task of examining them will not be easy, but productive tests are never easy. I have passed and failed hundreds of tests in my life and I have found that tests are necessary for successful living. ***Before you buy it—try it,*** is a good bit of advice.

Race relations are not just a national problem; they are current problems that nearly every community faces. Families often experience conflict over the race question too. During the Civil War families were torn apart. Some were Southern sympathizers, and some were Northern sympathizers. Brother fought brother. The Civil War is long gone, but racial conflict is still with us.

I could not understand how my father, who was the best man I ever knew, could be as prejudiced as he was. He did not see that he was prejudiced at all, and in many ways he was not. The attitude was hidden in the substrata of his culture and personality.

I often heard him tell jokes about blacks and laugh in great enjoyment. I called him on this, and he said he saw nothing wrong with having a little fun. He told jokes about Republicans, too.

I have heard it said that as a rule, the South hated black people as a category but often liked them as individuals. On the other hand, the North loved them as a category but hated them as individuals. It's so confusing.

Writing this book has been a test for me, too. I have written about Sociology, and taught many a course on the subject, but there are still few things of which I can be certain.

As I write this book I listen to the various candidates for president orate, and so much of what they say is about the problem of race. And I am sure that if we followed all of their prescriptions for solving the race problem in America, the country would surely break in two.

Recently a great article was published in *The Atlantic* —**The Black Family in the Age of Mass Incarceration**. It was a reconsideration of Senator Daniel Patrick Moynihan's book published 50 years ago—***The Negro Family***. Senator Moynihan's book was largely the foundation for much of the legislation passed by Presidents Johnson and Nixon. The use or misuse of Moynihan's book is the basis for many of the problems that we face today.

Today, I know much more about the race problem itself than I do about any viable solution. Like everyone else—both black and white—I have several solutions myself, and I can't wait until they are proposed so I can attack them.

One thing I think I know for sure is that the government has been one of the greatest contributor to the problem. It has been the author of laws and regulations that have created a wholesale dependency by the blacks on the federal government, and there is probably no way to escape that fact.

It is also greatly responsible for the criminalization of a vast portion of the black population. The statistics that are recorded about this phenomenon are frightening. And again, what has been done will be hard to back-track. Indeed, when the children of those who have already been incarcerated reach their teen years, we will actually see what we can't even imagine now.

Of course slavery has been a great contributor to today's problems. Perhaps, it's greatest evil is that it produced a breaking up of the black family. In doing that it reduced the authority of the father in each family and with the destruction of a strong father figure, the family as we know it collapsed.

The schools too, do not go blameless. They have produced an illiteracy among the black population that immunizes it from survival, let alone success.

Higher Education has been seized by a liberal establishment whose tentacles reach down into all levels of schooling. They also promote their product into business, politics, and even into the military. When I was a graduate student I read William Buckley's book ***God and Man at Yale***. Buckley was right.

The churches are also at fault. The established denominations have kept their antennas directed to the northeastern elite. Too often their dogma has even followed the money.

I don't want to get into the athletic problem, but many college and professional athletes are sad role models for young African-Americans. The same thing can be said about the entertainment industry.

There is probably nothing more contributory to our problems than public housing. I can't imagine the stupidity of our governmental leaders who hatched this rotten egg which is broken. And it stinks to high heaven. When will we ever learn that we should select our leaders based on character, morality, and competency and not on personality, popularity and appearance?

When I am elected president i will use executive privilege to create a Citizen Initiative College. I will make it mandatory for all youth to come under the control of this initiative until they reach the age of 20. Each person must enter programs that will promote basic citizenship and personal responsibility.

During World War II, one of the greatest soldiers was a cartoonist named Bill Mauldin. Bill published his cartoons in the GI newspaper ***Stars and Stripes***. When the war was over, he continued his career writing cartoons for a newspaper. Someone asked him what philosophy he used to draw his cartoons. He said my philosophy is... ***"If it is big—smash it."***

Therein lies the number one principle of my campaign for the presidency. If ***it is big—smash it.***

If the labor unions get too big, ***Smash them!***

If the political parties get too big ***Smash them!***

If the banks get too big ***Smash them!***

If the schools get too big ***Smash them!***

If the bureaucracies get too big ***Smash them!***

If congress gets too big ***Smash them!***

And, if taxes get too bigl ***Smash them!***

I will appoint a presidential commission—***Commission on Size***. And I will staff the commission with small people. Within a short time, I will come out with position papers on immigration, health care and guns. I will mail them to you on United States post cards.

Of course, if you agree with me, send me your vote and money. If it gets too big, ***I will Smash it***.

Snippets

What This Book Is Not About.

This book was written in southeastern Oklahoma where truth is direct and opinion is never hidden. Most conversations make sense, but a lot of it is just to fill up empty hours.

We do not have a **rush hour** down here. We're still looking for it. When we find it, we'll just wait for someone to come and tell us what to do with it. It sounds like this is a pretty dull place to live, but Oklahoma has never been a dull place to live. It has always been an exciting launching pad for those who love adventure. Just ask Will Rogers.

This book has not been a research report. It makes no claim to be a book that surveys the black experience, or the history of segregation. This book is not an academic exercise.

The book is not filled with analyses of black leaders or the various race laws and law suits. I really don't know much about all the actions of The Supreme

Court or of national and state laws which have been enacted.

Rather, this book has been somewhat of a memoir or perhaps it is more of a **case study** of race problems. I do believe that my experiences can assist in giving some measure of understanding to the problems that some have ignored and of the problems that we can ignore no longer.

The span of my attention extends from my boyhood to my geekhood. In dog years that is about 500 years. Don't even try to do the mathematics of that factoid.

I Made You a Semi-promise.

On the cover of this book I sort of promised you that I would answer the question "Are white people more prejudiced than black people?" To be honest with you I did not know the answer to that question when we were planning the cover, and to be honest with you, I don't have a good answer ***now***, even after spending hours writing this book.

Actually, the question was somewhat of a ***come-on***. What I really wanted to do was to feed you a lot of information to stimulate an answer from ***you***. In the meantime I have asked this question to many friends and strangers. Everyone that I have talked to has a good firm answer. I wish that I did. I still don't know and probably no one knows.

If you asked me that question on an important test that I was taking, I would probably fake an answer since that is all I have. I suppose there is some difference in the answers that Southern rebels will give you, from the answer that some yawning Yankees will give.

My guess is that the truth is out there somewhere on a continuum. In all probability it is not just sitting on an immobile line—it is moving—gradually and slowly, but it is moving.

Frankly, I think that just as the southern negro left the rural plantation for the local town and then left the rural town for the urban ghetto, the common opinion has become that there is probably more prejudice within the black community of the urban ghetto, than there was within the rural community of the old plantation. (Wow that last sentence nearly did me in.)

From what I am learning, prejudice may be growing faster in the urban ghetto, than it is in the mainstream of the white community.

But let's not argue about it. There is enough prejudice to go around for all of us. There is no shortage at all.

It is like a commodity, when there is a scarcity the price is high, and when there is an abundance, the price is low. Now if you can understand that sentence, write me and interpret it for me. I really would like to resolve this question once and for all.

I Gave my Students a Test

I remember teaching a beginning class in Sociology in which very early on the topics of class and caste were covered. I proposed the simple classifications of **lower**, **middle**, and **upper**.

Then I instructed the students to take out a piece of paper and determine the class of a fictional family. First I told them the man of the house was an engineer with a salary and bonus of $300,000 a year. His wife was a gynecologist and made about the same amount. Their oldest son was studying law at Harvard and the daughter was entering Smith.

Then I said to rank this family by the classification system of **lower**, **middle**, and **upper**. I told them to write their answers on the paper. and sign their names to it. And then acting like I had forgotten something, I said, "wait. I forgot to tell you they are a black family. Now look your answer over and if you want to change anything do it before you turn your paper in to me."

Immediately, it was obvious that most of the students were busily erasing their answers and substituting different answers for the ones that they had first put down."

Of course, I then announced that we all knew what was being erased and what was being written down, because we were all prejudiced in those secret moments. It was written into our DNA when no one was looking.

I confess I have been trying to erase that out of my DNA for 60 or 70 years, but sometimes I can still see a smudge of it lurking just under my arm pits.

I Love Adventure

Since this book has been offered as a ***case study,*** please go with me through some highlights of my journey. Every step of my journey has been a great adventure.

My boyhood was a great adventure and I loved every minute of it. I played *cops and robbers, cowboys and Indians* and *Yanks and Nazis*. My heroism in all of the battles struck fear in the heart of my best friend, Dean Wilmoth. Some 80 years later we still have our skirmishes, but mostly we just sit and reminisce. Of course, we were both wounded many times and we still have the scars to remind us of the battles of our youth.

But youth passes quickly, and before we know it we are in those reality years. The fun and games of youth were gone.

I was in my mid-twenties when war again knocked on the door of America. At that time the papers were full of the stories of three young men in Cuba who were leading a revolution against the Batista dictatorship in Cuba. Fidel Castrp, his brother Raul, and Che

Guevara were the Robin Hoods of my era and they had guns—not arrows.

During the 1960s the Congo massacres were in the headlines of the world's newspapers. I decided to go see the carnage myself. The trip into the Congo was uneventful, but, on the way out I ran into a guerilla action and barely escaped with my life.

One of the highlights of living in Africa was a visit that I took to a leper colony in Swaziland. I toured the small leper village as a guest of the director of the colony. The picture of dozens of natives who had been tortured by leprosy is seared on my brain forever. Luncheon served to me by lepers was not one of my most enjoyable dining experiences.

I was in Saigon in the early days of that dreadful war. I went as a civilian—not as a soldier. I wanted to see if it was as bad as the newspapers said it was. The slit trenches near the sidewalks announced that you could expect an enemy plane to bomb or strafe the area at any time. I didn't get strafed but I narrowly missed the bombing of the Army Officer's hotel next door.

In South America I visited the site where seven American missionaries were killed by native head-hunters on the shores of the Amazon river. In

Ecuador. A side trip led to hunting alligators at midnight. A couple of missionaries assured me that it was completely safe and it was. We caught three alligators, and ignored the thousands of piranha.

The Six-Day-War between Israel and Egypt is one of History's great events. I decided to see it for myself and visited Israel the week after the war was over. I decided to go down the road to Jericho. I didn't see a single good Samaritan, but I did see a couple of Israeli tanks still smoldering on the battlefield. I avoided a rocket attack at the Sea of Galilee one late night. I love adventure.

I will never forget visiting the upper regions of Mozambique where lions and mambas are a constant threat. Natives live in constant fear of their lives in that harsh environment.

On the road to Victoria Falls in old Rhodesia, a student and I were attacked by three giant bull elephants. Our small Volkswagon sputtered slowly away from the danger. I guess you could call me an adventurer. . . . . with a definite cowardly bent.

But those sorts of adventures are behind me. Now my adventures are mostly memories. That is not to say that I am inactive. I'm not. In the past dozen years I have built a dozen houses and written several books.

And trying to keep my younger wife happy is a full-time job.

I still have more ideas buzzing around in my head than I can capture. To accomplish just half of them will mean I will not be able to die until I'm 125 years old.

Even then, I will be writing another verse to one of my poems. Here is an appropriate one.

Why Do I Have To Leave?

Last evening, I sat in my chair and
looked out at the magnificent trees
mirrored on the water below

Beyond, the blue sky spanned the plains and
reached for the mountains so far away
I thought, how beautiful the world
and, the moment to enjoy it

In the deep silence it occurred to me
that in a few days, a few months
perhaps a few years
I will no longer exist to enjoy such beauty

With only a touch of sadness, I breathed a poem.

Why do I have to leave?
Only now have I discovered
The proud beauty of a tree
The waltz of heron over water
The grace of a reed in the wind

Why do I have to leave?
I've only begun to know
That wisdom, like a seed, grows
That truth is power enough
That wealth is a smile on your face

Why do I have to leave?
The worst is now behind me
The fickleness of desire
The transience of fame
The foolishness of treasure

But ah, it now occurs to me
That HERE is not heaven
NOW is not eternity

The mirror is dark for only a moment, and then
My gain will be greater than my loss
My limitations will no longer bind my soul

Yes, now it occurs to me
my soul is ready to soar.

Acknowledgements

Three of my former college classmates helped with this book. We first came together 70 years ago at a small denominational college in Oklahoma. We all left college to pursue educational careers. We still meet as we can since one lives in Colorado, one lives in California, and two of us stayed in Oklahoma to continue to enjoy the high life that Oklahoma provides us.

Dr. James D. Hamilton
Seminary professor.

Dr. Val Christensen
chemist and University Administrator.

Dr. Forrest Ladd
psychologist and University Administrator.

If you find any point of inspiration or wisdom in this book it was probably suggested by one of them. If you run into any section that is soggy or messy—the **mire** is all **mine**.

Books by

Kenneth Shelby Armstrong

— — —

Will it Be Dangerous?

Will it be dangerous? Could I get killed? These two questions plagued Dr. Armstrong as he enrolled in an all-black university as the only white student in the entire school. Murder was not the outcome but it was no romp. As a white student he received the kind of treatment at Atlanta University that black students received at Mississippi, Alabama, Texas and other southern universities. Later he went to Africa and taught at an all-white college and no blacks were allowed. You will be amazed as you read his other adventures.

Available at: www.Amazon.com Go to: Books and enter Kenneth Shelby Armstrong and the title of this book. It costs $7.99. www.WinWithWisdom.com

— — —

What Ever Happened to Robin?

On the sandy shores of Lake Biwa in Japan, a distinguished American bishop laid his head in the lap of a beautiful Japanese woman and died. His death revealed a secret that he had held since he was a young soldier in Kyoto following the World War II American occupation of Japan. This is a historical romance that must be read.

www.WinWithWisdom.com

To be available in 2016, at: www.Amazon.com

— — —

How to Strive, Thrive and Stay Alive in Prison

Staying alive in prison is not an easy task. This year more than 2,000,000 men and women will go behind bars and fight for safety, meaning, and a bleak future. Some, on the other hand have found secrets to making the experience profitable. The stories told here will make you **fear** and in some cases—**cheer**.

Available at: www.Amazon.com Go to: Books

and enter Kenneth Shelby Armstrong and the title of this book. It costs $7.99. www.WinWithWisdom.com

— — —

My Very Best Stories

A regular feature published weekly in *The Hugo Daily News* is a column entitled, *In His Own Words*. This column consists of the short stories of Dr. Armstrong. These stories were so inspiring that the Editor suggested that they be put in book form. Readers of all ages will enjoy them.

Available at: www.Amazon.com Go to: Books and enter Kenneth Shelby Armstrong and the title of this book. It costs $7.99. www.WinWithWisdom.com

— — —

Made in the USA
San Bernardino, CA
21 February 2016